How t a Used Bookstore

Learn How to Dominate Online or With a Physical Location

Mia Bexley

Readers acknowledge that the author is not engaging in the rendering of legal, financial, medical or professional advice. The content within this book has been derived from various sources. Please consult a licensed professional before attempting any techniques outlined in this book.

By reading this document, the reader agrees that under no circumstances is the author responsible for any losses, direct or indirect, that are incurred as a result of the use of information contained within this document, including, but not limited to, errors, omissions, or inaccuracies.

Table of Contents

Introduction

Books. One thing that's for certain is that you and I both have a love for books. Here you are reading a book and here I am writing one.

There's just something so special about books, especially physical books. The way they feel in your hands, turning the page, the way they smell, it's all an experience in and of itself. Of course, you don't just have to enjoy books by reading them, you can also make money selling books and spreading joy to other readers.

That's what this book is all about. How can you turn your passion of reading books into something that you can do full-time? I'm not here to tell you that it will be easy, but by the end of this book you'll know what you need to do in order to be successful.

Right now, you might not be sure if this is something you even want to do. Maybe you're not sure exactly how you want to start your used bookstore business. Regardless, I'm going to walk you though the different options you have and what I think is best depending upon your current circumstances. This is going to be a fun journey, so let's buckle up and get started!

Chapter 1: Online, Pop Up Store, Brick and Mortar, or Hybrid?

So you want to start your own used bookstore, but how should you go about it? As it turns out, you have quite a bit of different options when it comes to running your own bookstore. You might have only thought about running a store with a physical location, but that's definitely not the only way you have to go about things. Here's a breakdown of each of the ways you can start a used bookstore:

Online

This is definitely going to be the easiest and simplest way to get started. It's also going to have the least amount of start-up costs associated with it as well. There's not going to be overhead for things like rent from your lease or having to pay employees.

All you have to do is get inventory or use inventory you already have and use online platforms to get exposure and sell your books. Creating a website in the beginning may not even be the best way to go about things when you're just getting started. The reason for this is because it can take a lot to market yourself.

It's either going to take a lot of time and effort or you're going to have to pay for traffic. Instead it's easier to leverage social media platforms, online groups, or online marketplaces. These are places where people are already looking for their next book to read.

All you have to do is show up with the book that someone is looking for and boom you've got yourself a sale. Running your business solely online will involve quite a bit of trips to ship off your books for delivery compared to someone simply coming up to the front counter to checkout. However, shipping off books isn't a complicated item to send off unlike other items that may be breakable or have an expiration date.

Pop-Up Store

A pop-up store is a retail store that only stays open for a short period of time, hence why it's called a pop-up store. Pop-up stores usually rent out a small section of another retail business and it's temporary. A pop-up store may not sound that appealing, and it's usually not going to be anyone's end goal.

However, that's not the point of a pop-up store. A pop-up store is usually there to try and cash-in on a current trend or to test the waters. This is the key when it comes to a used book store.

Creating a small pop-up store will allow you to test the area and market by dipping your toes in the water before you take a full plunge. This is very important because the most important thing when it comes to a retail store's success is their location. Businesses will typically have to commit to a multi-year lease when renting a physical location for the business.

This can be tricky if you're not quite sure of how good a location will be. However, a pop-up store is a good way to work around that issue. You'll be able to tell if you're in a good area for used books without having to commit to a multi-year lease right off the bat.

This could be the difference between success and failure because starting a retail store is expensive. It can be hard to recover from one bad mistake such as choosing a poor location for your store.

Brick and Mortar

This is what most people tend to think of when it comes to starting a used bookstore. It's for a good reason. What's better than being surrounded by books all day long?

Getting to be around the smell of books and around people who love reading and talking about books is truly magical. Not to mention the fact that you're getting paid to do all of this!

This is obviously way better than a typical 9-5 job where you sit at a desk all day completing boring tasks.

Of course starting and running a brick and mortar location will not be easy. If it was easy, then everyone would be doing it. It will take a lot of effort before you even officially open your doors for business.

However, having your own physical location will create an experience for yourself and your customers that can't be replicated online. There's something different about physically being around books and people in person that's hard to describe. Think about it, ebooks are obviously a thing, and they contain the same information that a physical book copy would contain.

However, I know for myself personally, I prefer a physical copy of a book over an ebook. I'm sure you have similar preferences if you're interested in starting a used bookstore. This isn't the type of business that you start because it will make you the richest person in the world.

This is a business you start because you're passionate about books. If you're not passionate about books, then opening a physical location is a waste of time because it simply will not work (more on this later).

Hybrid

Finally we have the hybrid model, which is simply where you combine having an online presence with a physical location. How you go about it can vary, but typically you'll have a physical location in addition to an online website with the same name as your brick and mortar. Customers can go online and order books that will be delivered to them or picked up from your store.

The hybrid model definitely gives you the most exposure and thus the best way to make money, but that doesn't mean you should jump right into it. Running a hybrid model can involve the most amount of work as you'll have to manage online orders in addition to running your physical location. This can be overwhelming if you're not prepared for it.

The last thing you want to happen is for customers to get upset because you're unable to keep up with orders coming in online. It's typically going to be better to have one or the other until your systems and processes are down pat. Then you can open up the second avenue once you're able to handle it.

So Which Way Should You Start Your Business?

There really is no one-size fits all answer to this question. The answer for you will differ from someone else, however there are some things you need to consider.

For starters, what is your level of experience when it comes to business in general?

Have you ever owned your own business before? Or have you always been an employee for someone else's company? Do you have any experience working for a bookstore as an employee?

How much risk are you willing to tolerate? These are some things you'll want to think about before you make your decision. Having a love for books is great, but running a business is an entirely different beast.

Your love of books will definitely take you far don't get me wrong. Your customers will be able to see your passion. You'll be willing to work hard and persevere during tough times because you're doing something you enjoy.

Unfortunately though, there's more to being successful in business than just having passion. You have to pick your location, pick your inventory, and hire staff. All of these things will cost you time and money and one bad mistake can run you out of business.

This is why if you don't have any previous experience running your own business I recommend starting off with an online approach. Use this time to start building up your inventory and sell books online using various methods such as social media and online marketplaces.

You don't need to create your own website to start selling books online.

That's why this is a very low risk way to get started with making money from used books. You won't have to quit your current job, and you can use this time to save money towards opening a pop-up store. Also consider getting a job or part time job at a used book store if possible.

This way you can see all of the ins and outs of how that store runs without having to take on any of the financial risk. How is the store set up? How knowledgeable and up-to-date are employees about current books?

What books are put on front display and why? Yes I totally understand the eagerness behind opening a brick and mortar bookstore right from the jump, but a little bit of patience can go a long way. Even if you don't get a job at a used bookstore, still visit other used bookstores and study them to try and find out why they do what they do.

Once you're ready, I would recommend taking things one step at a time. This would mean transitioning to a pop-up store, then brick and mortar and finally adding an online presence where you accept orders directly from your website.

Of course when you should make the transition will all depend on your level of risk tolerance. How much money are you willing to take out on a loan? Are you ready to quit your job and go all in?

Some people might be ready to do that from the jump and there's definitely something to that. You're never going to have all of the answers, so there's no point in waiting for the "perfect time." At some point you will have to take that leap of faith.

However, there is a difference between going into something haphazardly and with a smart game plan. This is why I say give yourself some time to save and plan appropriately. In the meantime, you can definitely make some good money selling solely online.

And who knows you might not be interested in opening a physical location, you may want to run everything online. The good news is that you don't have to make a decision right this second. Regardless of which path you decide to go down, throughout the rest of this book I'm going to cover both avenues.

This way you can feel confident that you're heading in the right direction, and you'll know what to do when the time is right for a physical location.

Chapter 2: How to Get Things Set Up

Opening a physical location for a bookstore doesn't just magically happen. There's some leg work that you have to put in to officially open for business. In this chapter you're going to learn the ins and outs of what you need to do before you open for business. Let's get started!

Forming Your Business

The first thing you'll want to do is officially form your business. There are a few different types of businesses such as a sole proprietorship, LLC, and corporation. You'll want to carefully consider your options here as this will affect your liability protection as well as how you are taxed.

For instance, with a sole proprietorship, you are your business. Therefore, if something happens, your personal assets will be at risk. It also is not going to be a good look when trying to get a loan for your business.

The good news about a sole proprietorship is that it's the easiest to set up and run. However, when it comes to running a used bookstore with a physical location, this isn't a realistic option. Customers will be coming in and out of your store and anything can happen.

It's best to keep your personal assets safe by forming an LLC or corporation. This will also allow you to be taken seriously by real estate agents or banks that you'll work with to get your business off the ground and running.

Insurance

As I just mentioned, when you're running a retail store anything can happen. You have to be prepared for the worst and this is why insurance is an absolute must. There are a few different kinds of insurance that you'll want to consider such as the following:

Liability insurance- this type of insurance will help protect you in various instances such as someone getting hurt while they were in your store.

Commercial property insurance- commercial property insurance can help to protect your business in the case of an unfortunate event. For example, let's say someone breaks into your store and steals some of your inventory. This insurance could help to cover the cost from the lost inventory. Maybe there's an earthquake and your shelving gets damaged during the disaster. These are the types of things commercial property insurance will cover.

Workers' Compensation Insurance- when running a used book store, it's not realistic to try and do everything by yourself. You're going to need the help of other people, which means you're going to have to hire employees. If an employee gets hurt while on the job, workers' compensation insurance can help to cover medical expenses and wages for the employee that was injured. One example, could be an employee falling off of a ladder while restocking a shelf. An event like this may seem unlikely, but you have to be prepared for anything. One bad event that you don't have coverage for could put you out of business. That's why it's better to be prepared for unforeseen events, even if they don't seem likely to happen.

Business Interruption Insurance- this type of coverage will help protect you if you're unable to continue running your business due to an unforeseen event such as a pandemic, fire, or flood. This can help to keep your business afloat while your store is being repaired.

These are some of the main types of insurance that you'll want to consider when opening a brick and mortar store. Obviously you're going to be paying more for insurance running a physical location when compared to an online store, but the importance can't be understated.

Business Plan

Creating a business plan is like having a game plan for what your business does and how it will operate. Having a business plan is important when applying for a business loan and it will also help you be as prepared as possible once your business officially opens. This may not seem necessary, but imagine a coach going into a sports game without a plan.

You don't want to be like that when it comes to your business. Here are some of the things that you should include in your business plan:

Executive Summary- think of this part of your business plan as kind of an overall summary of what your business does and how it's unique. You'll explain specifics of your business more in depth in other parts of your plan, but this part is more so like a general overall summary.

Market Analysis- this is where you will do market research and find out what your competition is like in the surrounding areas. You'll want to be sure to include a section where you explain how your used book store will be unique or offer a competitive edge over other book stores in the area.

Finances- this is where you'll talk about projections of what you think your company will earn revenue wise. You can project one year out, 3 years, or even 5 years. Make sure you include projections for each year though. It's important to remember that these are simply educated guesses based on your analysis of the competition. You're not basing anything off of actual numbers.

Business description- this section is pretty self explanatory. You're simply going to describe what exactly it is that your business does and what makes it unique. You can also include a mission statement here and any core values that your company holds.

There are plenty of other things that you could include in your business plan, but it's better to keep things simple rather than complicated. Keeping things simple doesn't mean that it should be something you fly through without any thought. Again this is something that's part of the planning phase of your business.

This is also something that banks will want to see before they loan you any money. Therefore, take your time with it and think from the perspective of someone else reading your business plan. By the end of your business plan, someone should know exactly what you do and your plan to succeed without being confused.

That's why it's a good idea to get some of your friends or family members to read over your plan before you go asking for a loan. This way you can make any necessary tweaks along the way.

Location

Once you've finished your business plan, the next thing you're going to want to do is find a prime location for your business. This is something that will make or break your business so you're not going to want to take this step lightly. Obviously there are a lot of different factors that will determine a prime location such as competition and price.

Before I get into competition or pricing, let's talk a little bit more about location. You want to make sure you find a good area for your store to be in. It needs to be an area where there are a lot of people who will be passing by either on foot or in their cars.

It also needs to be easy to spot and access. This one is huge. Just think of this for yourself personally.

Maybe there's a certain gas station that you usually go to. Then one day construction started in that area and now the gas station is harder to access so you simply go somewhere else. Or maybe there's a certain business you drove past dozens of times without noticing it until finally something random made it catch your attention.

The point is that location matters a lot. People act out of convenience. Someone is really going to have to want to check out your bookstore if it's hard to get to.

People who are simply just curious aren't going to go out of their way to stop by and take a look. Remember that know one knows who you are. Therefore, you have to think of your store as a billboard that's constantly advertising for your business.

It's constantly letting people know who you are and that you exist. If you have a billboard in the middle of nowhere, it's pointless. It doesn't matter how cheap it is, it's still a waste of time.

The same goes for your store. You can't be solely focused on the price of the lease. If you're too worried about that, then it's a sign that you need to wait for a physical store or get comfortable with taking out a loan.

A prime location is going to cost more than an average spot, but again this will make or break your business so you have to take it very seriously. This is where working with a commercial real estate agent can come in handy. They'll be able to help you locate a spot for your store.

You can then tour the location and see if you think it'll be a good fit. Once you've toured a spot, you'll want to be sure to check out the surrounding area. How busy is the area?

What kind of other stores are located around you? For example, it can be a big plus if you're in the vicinity of a coffee shop because people enjoy reading books while drinking a coffee. This way you're fitting right in without having to put forth any extra effort.

Another thing you'll want to be on the lookout for is competitors that are in the area. Seeing someone else in the same area with a bookstore isn't the end of the world. You'll just want to ensure that you have a way that you stand out from that competition.

For instance, if the other bookstore on the block strictly handles new books, then you'll be able to appeal to a different audience by offering used books. Your books will be at a cheaper price, and customers who are looking for a certain older or niche book will be more likely to find it at your shop, then at a new bookstore. If a location checks all of the boxes, but there's another used bookstore in the same area, it doesn't have to be a deal breaker.

For one thing, there are more or less book stores depending on where you live to begin with.

Certain cities are going to have a bigger book reading community than others. So if demand is higher, then this also means that supply will be higher which means more competition.

You simply have to determine what your unique competitive advantage is over other used bookstores in your area. A good way to do this is to be better than your competition in a way that your customers can't ignore. For instance, if your book selection is consistently better, then it's a no brainer for people to buy from your store.

Keep popular books stocked up. Be willing to pay a little bit more for used books than your competitors and people will pick you over and over again. If you and your workers are more knowledgeable about certain authors and genres, then people will come back for more good recommendations.

You also want to think about the aesthetic and design of your store. Is it welcoming and inviting? Do the colors of your store go well together? If you store looks and feels like a messy place to be in people will not want to stay or come back.

What You Are

This leads me to my next point about designing your store, which is that you need to remember what you are. You sell used books. People who come to your store are people who come because they can find good books.

They don't come to your store because they can get the best coffee or find cool board games. Yes there are other book retailers out there who have success with selling a variety of other items, but that doesn't mean that you should follow suit. These companies are much more established than you are.

They have more experience and data to help them make informed decisions about what to stock their shelves with and what not to. You have to remember that you're only going to have so much square feet to work with. Every square foot that's taken up by something such as a board game is one less square foot for books.

More than that, it's about being focused on what your store is all about anyways which is books. This is what you know the best and it's what people will know you for too. You're going to have enough on your plate as it is when you're starting out so don't add in extra stress from trying to include a coffee bar or pastries or anything like that.

Focus is going to be your friend in the beginning. This isn't to say that you can't expand into other things such as board games or a coffee bar later on, but do so once you're more established. Keep things simple in the beginning and work your way up.

How Long Should Your Lease Be?

Okay so once you've found a location you think is solid, the thing you have to worry about is lease terms. Your real estate agent will be able to communicate what kind of terms the landlord is looking for. The shorter the lease is, the more you're going to pay per month.

The longer the lease term is, the less you're going to pay per month. Some landlords might only be interested in offering a longer-term lease such as 3-5 years to help provide more stability. It might be difficult to find a short-term lease or month-to-month option depending on the area.

It all comes down to the level of risk you're willing to take. If you find the perfect spot and the landlord wants a 5-year lease, you have to do what's best for your business. If you truly believe that you can succeed in this spot, then take the plunge if you feel that you're ready.

If you feel more hesitant, then that's totally cool. Remember you have other options so that you can test things out before diving in head first. Try out a pop-up store in that area and see how that goes first.

This will allow you to gain some confidence and make it easier to move forward with a decision to commit to a longer-term lease.

If your pop-up store doesn't do too good, then at least you were able to learn a lot, without it wrecking your business. You can then try another pop-up store in a different location and see how that goes. In the end, it's all up to you and the level of risk that you feel comfortable with.

Getting Financed

Once you've found a good location for your store, the next thing you may have to consider is financing. How much you need to be financed will of course all depend on your current financial situation. When starting a brick and mortar store, you have to have money to pay the rent every month, pay any employees you hire, shelving, inventory, and insurance among other things.

This can add up to quite a bit of money so getting financed makes sense. However, this doesn't mean that getting the necessary loans you need will just be handed over to you because you asked. Banks can be very selective with who they lend their money out too and for good reason.

They don't know who you are. They don't know your drive and your passion about books. They can only go off of the information that you tell them.

At the end of the day, the bank is a business too. If they repeatedly give out loans that get defaulted on, then they will go out of business. So don't take things personally if it's a little more challenging to get the money you need than you first thought.

This is where something such as having your business plan will be needed. It'll show them the type of business owner you are. It shows them that you have a plan in place to succeed.

However, that's not all that they'll want to see. Having a plan in place is awesome, but they'll likely want to see some credit history as well. If you're just starting your business, then you won't have a business credit history.

This can really hurt you because a bank would like to see proof that you have a history of paying back money that your business has borrowed. This is another point where starting with a pop up store makes sense. The overall costs will be lower, and it will be easier to get financed.

Once you get financed, you'll then be able to start paying back the loan and start building up your business credit history. Regardless of what type of store you open first, you're going to start out with no business credit history. Banks may want to see your personal credit history and use that to help them decide if handing you a loan is a good idea.

A bank may offer you a loan, but they may want you to put up personal assets as collateral. If you were to default on your loan, the bank would then be able to possess the assets that you put up. Putting up collateral can be scary and it all comes back down to the level of risk that you're willing to take.

Again if you're not comfortable with taking much risk right now, that's totally cool. Remember you can always start off online where the start-up costs are way cheaper.

Crowdfund Campaigns

One way that you can raise some money without having to take on the risk of a standard loan is via crowdfunding. Essentially this is where a group of people will give money towards a campaign of some project. You'll use a crowdfunding website to post about your project and people will be able to give money towards the project.

Of course people aren't just going to want to put money towards your project for nothing. Typically people who donate towards a project will be given some type of reward or incentive for doing so. For a physical product this could be something such as receiving an early prototype, a discount on the product once it's finished, or some other type of perk that will make people want to give towards the cause.

In the case of crowdfunding for a physical store, things will be different because only people in the area will get to see the finished store. If you want to be able to appeal to people across the county, you have to get creative to find a way to make it worth their while. This could be something such as a gift card for your online website that goes alongside your store once the time comes for that.

It could be a free copy of a book that you've written. Crowdfunding isn't going to be easy, but it's a different option that you can explore so at the very least you can take out less money from a traditional loan. It's easier to have a successful crowdfund campaign if you have an engaged social media following.

This way you have an audience you can immediately appeal to as soon as your campaign starts. If you don't have a good following, you can start online only at first to help build your following and thus make it easier to crowdfund when the time comes. If not, then your best chances of success are going to be having a good incentive for people and/or coming up with something that makes your campaign compelling.

For instance, this could be the story behind why you're starting a bookstore. If you talk about the adversity you've overcome in your life to get to where you are now, you could better your chances of moving someone to contribute.

What if I want to Start Out Online?

If you're interested in starting off online only in the beginning, then there's a lot less that you have to worry about when it comes to getting everything set up. You're not going to have to worry about finding a physical location, paying monthly for a lease, employees or anything like that. Essentially what I'm getting at is that there's going to be a lot less overhead expenses that you have to worry about when it comes to being strictly online only.

Even though you'll be operating by yourself, you still need to consider if you want to start out as a sole proprietor or an LLC. You also won't need nearly as much insurance as you would with a physical store. It all comes down to the level of risk that you're comfortable taking on.

Having an LLC will help to protect your personal assets and it's not a bad idea to have general business liability insurance. That's all you're really going to need in order to officially set up your business online. From there it's simply about expanding your inventory, which I'll cover more in depth here shortly.

Finally, you just need to start marketing about your books so your potential customers can know that you exist in the first place.

You'll want to make sure that you create social media accounts for your business so that you can start building up a loyal following. In the meantime, you'll still have plenty of options to market your business.

You'll definitely want to use this time to learn as much as you can. This way you'll be able to determine when and if transitioning into a physical store will make sense to you. If you are interested in starting up a physical location one day, consider getting a job at a used bookstore.

This will help you to learn a lot of the day-to-day operations for free. This is much better than trying to learn on the fly after you've fully committed to a lease.

Chapter 3: Where Should You Get Your Books From?

Getting books is obviously a very important part of your business. If you don't have books to sell, then you have no business. You might already have a pretty large personal book collection, however if you want to be successful, you're going to have to have a multitude of ways to get books.

You'll need to have access to a wide variety of genres and newer and older books so that you can appeal to more people. Who knows someone just might have bought a certain book from you if you had it in stock. That's not something you're going to want to experience on a regular basis.

Therefore, it's going to be really important that you stay on top of sourcing new books to sell for your business. Think of it like a college football team. Yes the coaches have to stay focused and do what they can to win games this season. However, that's not all that they have to think about.

They also have to be focused on bringing in new recruits for the following season. Not recruiting won't have a noticeable impact on their current season, but it will soon become apparent in the following season and the season after that. The same goes for selling books.

You may have a great selection of books right now, or you'll have a solid collection before you open. That's only the beginning, if you stop trying to get new books, you'll soon be left with a sparse amount of books left to sell.

Getting Books as a Brick and Mortar

Most of the methods that I'm going to share for getting books will work regardless of whether or not you're only online or have a physical location. This method that I'm about to share with you is exclusive for a physical location. It's nothing groundbreaking and it's something that just about every used book store will offer.

This is where you'll pay your customers money to buy their books off of them. This is a great strategy because people are coming to you with books. You don't have to put in time and effort into hunting down books like you will with some of these other methods.

However, just because people are bringing you books doesn't mean that this method is foolproof. Remember if you're running a brick and mortar, you only have so much shelf space to begin with. You only have so much spare capital to be able to buy books with.

This is why you have to be picky when it comes to what books you buy and how much you're willing to pay for them.

As soon as you buy a book from someone, it now becomes your job to sell that book. Every day that book sits on the shelf is costing you money.

Ultimately, if you're able to buy back the right kind of books and hit a sweet spot with how much you're paying for these books (more on this later), then you'll create a circular effect. People will bring you inventory. You'll then sell that inventory to other people.

Some of these people will even bring back books that they bought from you so that they can get more money for other books. The cycle will then continue from there. You can even offer an incentive for people to use your book buying program more often.

For instance, you can give them a cash offer or you can give them a store credit offer that's worth more than the cash offer. You can also create a rewards program where customers earn points based on the number of eligible books that they sell to you. The beautiful thing about a physical store location is that you can really use this method to your advantage.

You're not going to have to constantly hunt down books on your own all of the time. It's going to allow you to be able to focus on other things in your store. Of course in the beginning if you still need to expand your inventory, relying on this alone may not be enough.

You'll definitely still want to stay on top of the other methods listed below to ensure that you always maintain a strong inventory. Nobody wants to go to a bookstore that looks barren and sparse.

Getting Books as an Online Bookstore

The following methods are going to be more of a manual process to getting books than the method listed above for a brick and mortar store. However, don't let that scare you. Things aren't going to be a walk in the park in the beginning.

Think of things like a treasure hunt. It's exciting to go searching for books because you never know what amazing things you'll be able to find.

Garage Sales

One of the first places that you can find some good deals on books will be garage sales. People who sell books as part of a garage sale will typically get rid of large collections at a time. This gives you a great opportunity to buy quite a bit of books at once and for a great price.

If someone is selling a large number of books at a garage sale, chances are good that they're not going to be able to sell all or most of their books. This is where you can come in and get a great deal. You can offer to buy as many of the books that make sense for your business and even bargain with the person running the garage sale.

If you're not able to get a deal that you think is fair, don't be afraid to come back later in the day. As time goes on, the person running the garage sale will be more likely to offer a better price since they'll likely just want to move on from any items that they can. This is typically the mentality of most people who run a garage sale.

They want to get rid of some items that they don't want anymore and if they can get some money out of it then great. The trick is going to be finding garage sales. Typically people will host garage sales on a Saturday.

It can be worthwhile to drive around some neighborhoods to see what you can find. The best bet is when communities host a garage sale. Essentially a lot of people in a neighborhood will have a garage sale on the same day.

These garage sales bring out a lot of people because everyone who lives in that neighborhood will know that there will be a lot of people who have a garage sale on that day. This will be a good opportunity to get books. So be sure to stay on top of your own community's announcements via social media or that of other communities around you.

You can also search online for garage sales around you to help make this process more streamlined.

Flea Markets

Finding good books at a flea market is a similar process to that of a garage sale. The major difference is that you're not going to be driving around neighborhoods. Instead you go to one location where a bunch of vendors will be who are looking to sell their products.

Chances are good that you'll be able to find a few vendors who are looking to sell some of their books. Again this is a great opportunity to find some great books. Just like with a garage sale, you can bargain for a better deal if you want to.

If you want to buy a large quantity of books from someone, you could ask for a discount. You could even come back again towards the end of the day to see if the vendor is more willing to budge on pricing. I would still recommend that you go to the flea market earlier in the day so that way you can have first dibs on any potential rare finds.

If you're looking for a better deal for buying in bulk, you're more likely to achieve success later on in the day when the vendor is tired and just trying to get rid of inventory. In the area that I live, there are four different towns that alternate hosting a flea market on each Saturday of the month. So I have the opportunity to go to a flea market every Saturday if I want to.

The same could be for you. Flea markets definitely aren't hard to find. You can quickly figure out where one will be in your local area by doing a quick online search.

Thrift Stores

Thrift stores can be a great resource for you to find good books. The cool thing about a thrift store is that they stay in the same location so you can easily check in every so often and see if there's anything good. This is definitely better than going on the hunt to even find a garage sale only to hope that the person is selling books.

You may not find any good books at the first thrift store you go to, but at least you'll easily know where to find it. Quite a few people aren't going to like the idea of hosting a garage sale and sitting around all in the hopes that someone will buy their stuff. Instead it's easier for them to take their used items to a thrift store directly and see what kind of money they can get for them.

Sadly, most people don't realize just how valuable some of their books can be. However, as sad as it might be, this provides a great opportunity for people who are starting a used bookstore. Unlike with a flea market and garage sale, you won't be able to bargain for a lower price, but that really doesn't matter.

Chances are good that any books you'll find will be at a great price point. In the beginning it's worth hitting up as many thrift stores as you can at least once per week to help you start to build up a strong amount of inventory.

Online Marketplaces

Online marketplaces are going to be one of the easiest places to find great deals on books or bundles of books. You'll easily be able to search for books from the comfort of your own home. Similar to the other methods listed so far, people typically want to clear out some of their old stuff and make a few bucks rather than just donating items.

This is where a perfect opportunity comes in for you because you can look for books at anytime. If you're still working a 9-5 job, you can look for books during your spare time at work and go and pick up the books after work if the person is local. Some sellers may ship the books to you depending on what website it is that you're using.

Either way, it would be a good plan to use your time throughout the week looking online for used books. Then on Saturdays you could go around hunting for books at garage sales, thrift stores, and flea markets.

Donations

Believe it or not, donations can actually be a good way to get some books for free. This can especially be true if people know that you're starting a used bookstore. If you know of friends or family who have a large collection of books that they no longer want or need, why not ask them to make a donation for the launch of your used bookstore?

You could also make a post to your personal social media accounts asking if anyone would be willing to make a donation of any unwanted books for the start of your used bookstore. This can also work as a good word of mouth marketing tactic too. If someone donates books to you, they'll be more likely to tell their friends about your store because some of their books will be part of your inventory.

They'll feel like they contributed and had a special part in getting your bookstore started. The thing with this is that you can't be picky. You have to take any books that someone offers you.

Being picky can make you come across as ungrateful and the person might not want to give you anymore books in the future or recommend you to their other friends. Just because you take books, it doesn't mean you have to try and sell every book you receive. Some books are unlikely to garner much of any interest or be unsellable due to their condition.

If you're short on space, you may have to donate or sell these extra books at a second store that would be willing to take them. This of course isn't the only way that you can receive donations. Remember you're also going to have business social media accounts.

You can use these social media accounts to ask your followers for any donations of books that they no longer want or need. This alone may or may not get you very good results. However, you can take things one step further to gain more interest.

As part of your social media, you should do reviews on books and give recommendations to your followers. This will help them to make informed decisions about what they should read next. And they might just try and get that book from you!

So you can offer a shout out to the person who donated the book that you review. People love being acknowledged and this is a great way to show some love to your followers who are helping out your business. To use this same premise with a physical location, you could put up a tiny display or note stating who the book was donated by.

Most of your books will be lined up on shelves, but some of the best sellers will be on display.

You could use this tactic for books that are set up on a display to encourage other people to want to donate their books for the potential of being recognized.

These are some of the main ways that you can get books for your bookstore. Sourcing books at thrift stores or flea markets isn't always going to be the most fun thing, but it's part of the process of getting started. You'll seriously get such a big rush when you come across a great find because that's money in your pocket.

Yes it might be easier to try and find books at a secondhand store, but remember other bookstores are businesses too. They're trying to make money so you're already going to have to buy the book at a decently high price and then mark it up even more in order to make a profit on it. It certainly is going to require more effort to go around to different places to hunt down books, but it will be worth it in the end.

Getting to be around books all day is the ultimate goal so just always keep that in mind when you're doing some part of the business that you may find to be a little tedious.

Chapter 4: How Should You Price Your Books?

One thing you have to take into consideration when it comes to starting a used bookstore is the price of your books. This is a major step that you have to think really hard about because it can make or break your business. If you price your books too low, you'll leave money on the table and hurt your profits.

If your prices are too high, you could find yourself losing out on customers because they might as well go somewhere else or buy the book new. So in this chapter, my aim is to help give you some direction as to how you should go about pricing your books.

How Much Should You Sell Your Books For?

Let's first talk about how much you should charge for your books if you're running a physical store. When you're running a physical store, your overhead costs are going to be much higher than a store that's purely online. You must take into consideration your overall monthly expenses and use that to determine what kind of a profit you want to make on each book that you sell.

Most retail stores operate at a 40-50% profit margin. So in your case, if you paid $5 for a book, then you would want to resell that book for somewhere between $8.33-$10. This may not seem like a lot of profit but you have to keep in mind that you're selling books.

Books are relatively low in cost compared to other items such as buying a car or a house. A book is something that people will buy more frequently. When it comes to items that you'll sell more frequently, the amount of money that you make per sale will be less, but you'll sell more items overall.

Conversely, people don't buy cars that often, but when someone does buy a car, the amount of profit will be much higher due to the fact that it has to be to cover for all of the expenses that go into creating and selling a car. The amount of effort needed to sell a book is much smaller. The exact amount of profit margin you'll set will depend on your overhead costs, but if you want a good place to start, go ahead and aim for around 40-50%.

The reality is that you can always adjust your prices later on if you need to. Adjusting prices is something that scares many business owners and rightly so. They don't want price changes to potentially scare away customers.

The good news for you is that if you're just starting out, you don't have an established customer base. People won't be able to tell that you've changed your prices because they're not established with your store. This is why I recommend that you start off on the higher end of that profit margin recommendation.

If sales aren't where you want them to be, you can always lower them and see if that will help to boost sales. It's better to start on the higher end and go lower rather than to start low and have to increase prices. Increasing prices is where costumes can get upset.

And since you'll be in business for a while before you likely make any noticeable changes to your prices, some of these customers may notice. It's better to give them a pleasant surprise with a lower price, rather than to surprise them with a higher price.

How to Price Books for an Online Store

If your store is solely online, then you can use a lower profit margin than a physical store due to having less overall expenses. Having less overall expenses also gives you the ability to hold onto inventory for a longer time as well if you choose to do so. This can be a good option to consider if your overall inventory is low.

With a low amount of inventory, you can set a higher price point and be more patient for it to sell. Making a higher profit margin is important if you don't have a lot of books to sell in the first place. You're also going to have to put in more work to acquire books when compared to a physical store that can have customers bring in books as part of a buy-back program.

If you set the price higher and it doesn't sell as quickly as you'd like, you can always adjust to a lower price point. A good profit margin average that online stores try to operate at is around 20% give or take. This means that if you acquired a book for $5, you would price the book at $6.25.

This allows you to sell used at a price point that is still profitable yet cheaper than what most physical stores will sell at. This is important because people tend to be less trusting of online sellers that they don't know when compared to a physical store. Again though, if you have a low amount of inventory, then start with a profit margin of 30-40% and drop your price if the book takes too long to sell.

You also have to take into consideration shipping costs. You'll want to make the customer pay for shipping costs because your profit on the book is already low enough as it is.

Should Pricing Structure Be the Same for All Books?

Now you might be wondering if you should follow the same rule of thumb for every book you come across. The answer to that is definitely not! The reason for this is because some books are going to sell way easier than others.

The suggestions I mentioned above are what I recommend for popular books or best sellers. The reason why is because these books will sell themselves. These books are well known amongst book readers and they're well marketed so people will be on the lookout for them.

If the cost of a new best seller is too much for someone, then they'll look to a secondhand store for a better deal, which is where you come in. These books won't last long in your inventory so you can afford to set a lower profit margin on them when compared to other books. You should constantly be cycling through acquiring popular books and selling them.

What about other books though? Not every book is a best seller and it doesn't make sense to stock your bookstore with nothing but best sellers. The reality is that people love to read from certain genres.

People love romance novels or science fiction among other things. Therefore, you'll still have people come into your store looking for their next good romance novel that they can read or whatever genre it is that they prefer. So how do you go about pricing these kinds of books?

For books that aren't best sellers, you'll want to buy them at a lower price and have a higher markup on them. The reason for this is because these books will likely take longer to sell when compared to a best seller. Therefore, you'll want to capitalize on any particular book when it does sell.

You'll also be acquiring general books at a much lower price point when compared to books in high demand. This affords you to still be able to price a book at a cheap price and still make a good profit on it. For instance, you might buy a book for 60 cents and sell it for $3.00.

This would result in a net profit margin of 80%. This is obviously a quite higher margin than that of a best seller, but keep in mind the overall price for the book was $3.00. This is a great price for the customer, so price is not likely to be a deterring factor when it comes to selling less popular books.

The deterring factor is that the book isn't well known so it can take a while for a reader to potentially be interested in it and actually purchase it. You might be wondering how much you should buy books for to help you determine your price point, so let's dive into that now.

How Much Should You be Buying Books for?

If you're a physical store that offers customers the opportunity to sell their books to you, how much money should you give them? Well that's really going to come down to a few factors. The first is going to depend on what the book is.

If you're dealing with a best seller, you'll typically want to buy the book for 20-30% of what the book sells for brand new. This will typically depend on what the condition of the book is, as you'll obviously offer more money for a book that is in great condition. So for instance, if someone offers to sell you a popular book that is in a condition that looks like new, offer to buy the book for 30% of the new price.

So if the new price is $18, then you would buy the book for $5.40. This still gives you plenty of wiggle room to markup the book and resell it for less than what it would cost new. A 40% net profit on this book would sell for $9 and at 50% it would sell for $10.80.

Everyone wins in this scenario. The reader wants money because they no longer want to keep the book, so something is better than nothing. You get to resell the book to someone else and make money.

The person who buys the book from you is going to get a book in great condition for a price that is cheaper than brand new, so the end customer wins as well.

When it comes to non best sellers, you should simply put a rule of thumb in place. For instance, you might not offer to pay more than $3 for any book that isn't a best seller.

How much you'll pay will depend again on condition and popularity. If a book still has demand but isn't quite a best seller, then you can offer something on the higher end of your limit for what you're willing to pay. Conversely, books with a lower demand will garner a lower price point.

Typically people will come in with quite a bit of books and be happy with whatever you offer them because something is better than nothing to them. You can often offer less than a dollar for a lot of the books that you'll come across.That may not seem like a lot, but in reality it is.

These books are going to be harder to sell, so you're going to have to price them lower, which means you're going to have to offer less when buying them. You also don't have to pay out just cash for other people's books. You can also give them a store credit offer.

You'll want to ensure that your store credit offer is better than the cash offer otherwise no one will be interested in it. A good range is to offer 15-20% more for a store credit offer than what your cash offer would be.

So for instance if someone trades in books that equates to $100 for a cash offer, then you would also offer a store credit option of $115-$120.

The reason why this is important is because it ensures that all of the money the person receives will be spent with you over time. If the person takes the cash offer, it's highly unlikely that they will spend all of the money you gave them at your bookstore. With a store credit offer, you get the books up front which you can sell and make money from, and there's no guarantee that the customer will use up all of their store credit.

This is actually why businesses offer gift cards. It would seem like a pointless thing that you wouldn't make money on, but that's far from the case. When someone buys a gift card for let's say $20, the company gets all of that money upfront and some people don't get around to spending all of the gift card money.

They might lose it or receive it as a gift even though they don't like that store. This is how stores make a profit from gift cards. Even if all of the money is spent, it helps with cash flow because you get the entire sum of the gift card purchase right then and there which can then be reinvested back into the business.

And it's not like you're providing any "real" value in that moment like you would be if you sold a book that you would have to replenish.

Think of it like an I own you, except there's a chance that you won't have to owe the full amount back to the person.

Chapter 5: How to Market Your Business to Get Customers

When it comes to the success or failure of your business, there may not be anything more important than marketing. This is especially true if your business is solely online. If you're a brick and mortar, you can rely on your location in addition to how you market.

Regardless of being online or a physical location, you have to correctly position yourself and know how to get your name out there. There are tons of different ways that you could market your business. This doesn't mean that all of the methods are created equally though.

You have to be smart with the time and money you do have to market your business.

This is Fundamental

The first thing that I want to talk about is something that is foundational to your success regardless of what type of used bookstore you're running. That is the fact that you need to be knowledgeable and up-to-date with authors and genres. If someone comes to your store or messages you on social media, you need to be able to properly guide them to finding a book that is right for them.

Imagine what kind of a look you're creating for your business if someone asks for a recommendation and you stumble and struggle to help them out because you have no idea. If you're someone who regularly reads a wide variety of books and stays current with news about authors or other various books that are coming out, then you'll be good to go. All it takes is a reader having one positive experience with a book that you recommended for them to be hooked and keep coming back for more.

They'll also be way more likely to recommend your store to their friends and family. Just think of this from your own perspective. How would you feel if you went into a bookstore and asked for a recommendation and couldn't get the help you really needed?

You would probably be discouraged from going back. Bookstores that have been in business for a while know this and that's why they want their employees to be as knowledgeable as possible when it comes to the products that they're selling.

How to Launch Your Brick and Mortar or Pop Up Store

Okay this is a critically important step that you have to think about. You don't just want to open your doors and say, "Bam we're open!" You might find yourself disappointed with how much business you're leaving on the table.

You want to launch your business in a way that creates a lot of appeal for people to want to come and check it out.

This is your only opportunity to launch your store so you're going to want to make the most of it. Therefore, this is a unique situation where you can do things differently to get the ball rolling. You want to create a special offer that peaks people's interest so they'll come into the store.

This will likely be something where you'll either break even or possibly even lose a little bit of money on the offer you create. Losing some money on your special deal may seem counter intuitive, but what you're gaining in exchange is far more valuable. You're creating a strong wave for your store to ride right after you launch it.

You want as many people as possible to come by and check things out. If you're able to truly wow the people that come by, they'll be more likely to tell their friends and family and this is the impact that you want to create. Think of it like a restaurant or grocery store giving away free samples.

The store is losing money by giving the samples out for free. However, free samples work because people can sometimes be hesitant to spend money on something new they might not like. The free sample allows them to get over that barrier and if they enjoy the new product, they'll keep coming back for more time and time again.

So this one small investment can pay dividends for grocery stores and the same premise can work for you. In the case of launching your used bookstore, you could make a special offer such as buy three get one free or buy one get one half off. You could even run a promo for book trade-ins as well if you're in need of some extra inventory.

Having a special offer simply won't be enough though, people need to hear about the offer and if the offer is good enough, they'll come and check out your store. So how do you go about marketing the opening of your store? Well one of the best forms of advertisements for a physical store is going to be the store itself.

So why not use the location to your advantage? As soon as you possibly can, be sure to include a sign somewhere around your store letting people know what kind of store is about to open. Then a week before you're set to open, make a sign outside that lets people know what kind of a deal you're going to offer for your launch.

If your store is in a good location that generates a lot of foot traffic, this alone will help you gain quite a bit of interest. The second thing you'll want to be sure to do is leverage your own personal social media accounts. Your personal social media accounts will already contain friends and family members who want to support you because they like who you are as a person.

They could possibly share the post themselves or tell their friends about it in person. You never know how far one simple post can get you. If you already have an established business social media account, then you'll definitely want to make a post on those accounts as well.

Also whenever you make a post about your launch on your social media accounts, give people a reason to share the post. You're only going to be launching your store once, so you might as well make the most of it. For instance, you could say at the end of your post that you're offering a 20% discount coupon for anyone who shares this post.

This essentially has a double effect. People will share it, which will create more exposure. And then for the people who share it, it gives them a reason to come to your store and spend money with you.

Finally, don't be afraid to run some advertisements as well. Social media ads are very targeted nowadays. You can target people from a specific region as well as target people based on interests.

This means that you can show your ad to people from a specific town or city and only people in that town or city who have an interest in books. In your ad you'll want to make sure that you tell people about the special launch offer to increase the likelihood that someone will come by the day you launch. Even if people see your ad or post and don't come in for opening day, that doesn't mean you've failed.

There will be people who are busy that day and can't make it for one reason or another. However, they may still come by and check out your store some other time which is still a good thing. Sometimes when it comes to marketing you're not going to see immediate results, but it will pay off in the long run.

Think about it with a fast food ad. Do you see a fast food ad and immediately jump in your car and go to that place? No, of course not.

If the ad was compelling enough though, the thought of going to that fast food place will be in the back of your mind the next time you need a quick bite to eat. So even if it appears like your ad didn't do well, you have to keep in mind the long-term effect that it could have.

During your launch, you should have quite a bit of people come through your store, this is the perfect opportunity to offer them something unique that will keep them coming back for more.

For instance, you could create a live discussion that's hosted at your bookstore. You could center the discussion around a new popular book that recently came out or around a certain genre where people can talk about their favorite books from that genre.

Either way you want the event to be something special to give people a reason to sign up for the discussion while they're at your store for the launch. I know for myself personally after I read a good book, I want to talk about it. I want to recommend it to someone else or talk about it with someone who has read the book as well. Other people are the same way.

Meeting in person and talking about a book simply has a more potent effect than an online discussion board. So don't be afraid to offer a discussion event anywhere from once a month to once a week to get people to come to your store time and time again. You can also advertise in your store what book the upcoming discussion is going to be about.

People who see the ad might not come to the event and that's okay. The ad still might encourage them to check out a book that they otherwise might not have. People might think that if the book is good enough to be the center of a discussion, then it must be worth reading!

Marketing as an Online Store

When it comes to marketing as an online store, there are some things you can do that work well for both a brick and mortar and online store. For instance, you can also launch your online store using some similar methods to that of a physical store. You can launch with a special offer such as buy three get one free just like with a physical store.

You definitely should post about your upcoming launch and give people an incentive to share your post about your launch. However, once you're up and running, what is your day-to-day marketing plan going to look like? You have to continually put in effort to make your store known.

With a physical location, the store itself is a continual advertisement. If the location is good, that alone can be enough to generate customers consistently. With an online store, that's not the case.

People are only going to know about you if you tell them. This is why in the beginning if you're just starting out, I recommend that you lean heavily on selling your books on online marketplaces. The reason being is that if your inventory is small, someone who comes to your website might not like any of the books you have available to offer.

It's also going to be hard to generate enough traffic for your store to gain traction right from the start. Don't get me wrong, you'll still market your store and get eyeballs on your website, but it can be a gradual process to get it to take off.

An online marketplace can help you generate sales right from the start. The reason online marketplaces are so beneficial is because you're working with an established company. This company is a brand that people trust.

This company already has a lot of traffic coming through their website. All you have to do is show up with a book that people are already searching for on these online marketplaces. If you're able to do that, then sales will seamlessly happen.

The more books you have listed, the better your chances are of being discovered. You can then use earnings from these book sales to help out with some of these other marketing methods that I'm about to mention here.

These methods are online specific that can help you promote your online or physical store. The first one is to strategically use the power of other people on social media and the internet. Social media is full of people who run book blogs.

Essentially they review books that they read. Some of these people have quite a bit of followers as well. You might be wondering what that has to do with you. Well what you can do is offer to give a book blogger one of your books for free in exchange for a shoutout.

This strategy can work really well because the followers of this person are trusting of their opinion. If they recommend a book, they'll be inclined to want to check it out. You'll definitely want to have multiple copies of the recommended book in stock because people will come to check out your online store and potentially buy the book.

Even if people don't buy the recommended book, that's okay. They might buy something else and at the very least, you're gaining a ton of exposure to a brand new audience. It's really a win-win for both sides.

The book blogger is receiving a free book and you're getting some good advertising for your business. Now depending on how big the blogger is, you might have to do more than just giving the person a free book. You might have to pay them some money as well to get the shoutout that you're looking for.

Don't be intimidated by this because it's still worth the cost. You just have to make sure that you're getting promoted from the right blogger.

Looking at a blogger's followers simply isn't good enough.

A blogger could have just bought those followers so you'd essentially be wasting your time and money getting a shoutout from someone like that. Be sure you look at the engagement of the posts this person makes. Do their posts generate a lot of genuine comments?

Are these comments something that takes more than two seconds to type out? If people are going in depth with their comments on the posts this blogger makes, then it's a good sign that their audience is engaged. This is the type of person you want to get a shoutout from.

This strategy works great if you have an online store because the person's followers from anywhere in the country can visit your site. If you have a physical location, it can be a bit more tricky because someone who lives far away isn't going to go out of their way to check out your store. Your best bet is to find a blogger that is specific to the city that you live in.

This way it's more likely that some of their followers will also be from the same city and thus check out your store. You also want to make sure that you're posting regularly on your social media accounts regardless of what kind of a store you are. Every time you post is essentially free exposure so you might as well take advantage of it as much as you possibly can.

I recommend posting a minimum of 3 times per week but try to post at least 5 times per week. In terms of what you should be posting, you can post about a variety of different things. You could post about new books that you have in your inventory, book sales or promos that you're offering, and even do reviews for books that you've previously read.

The benefit to doing reviews is that your followers are looking for their next good book to read and they might buy a book you recommend from your store. Ultimately in terms of getting your online store off the ground, it's going to take quite a bit of manual effort. You're going to be interacting with a lot of book bloggers.

You're going to be posting a lot as well. Don't let that deter you. Just stay focused on online marketplaces in the meantime while you get things going. Perseverance is the key to success with this!

Conclusion

You now have the knowledge to get started with your online bookstore. The best thing you can do if you plan on opening a physical store is to spend quite a bit of time on the location of your store. It really is that important.

If your store is online, focus on building up your inventory and marketing as much as you can to build up your business. Owning your own bookstore isn't going to be easy and that's okay. If it was a walk in the park, then you'd see people opening up stores left and right.

All I can tell you is that it will be worth it. The feeling of owning your own business is like no other. There will be hard times, but preserving through those times is well worth it. Remember why you started in the first place.

This business gives you the freedom to do things the way you want to. It gives you the ability to be in more control of how much you make. And best of all, you get to be around books all day. So what could be better than that?

Printed in Dunstable, United Kingdom

72384847R00037

THE OLDEST GIRL

THE OLDEST GIRL

Aileen La Tourette

Caliband Books

First published in Great Britain in 2011 by
Caliband Books
77 Dunbridge Street, London E2 6JG

Printed in Latvia

A catalogue record for this book is available from
The British Library

ISBN 978-0-907633-91-4